Spread the Word

How to promote nonprofit groups with a network of speakers

by Terri Horvath

First Edition

Publishing Resources,
A division of The Resource Group,
Indianapolis, Indiana

Spread the Word

How to promote nonprofit groups with a network of speakers

by Terri Horvath

Published by Publishing Resources,
a division of The Resource Group
9220 N. College Avenue
Indianapolis, IN 46240-1031

All rights reserved. No part of this book may be reproduced or transmitted by any form or by any means, electronic or mechanical, including photocopying, recording or by any information storage and retrieval system without written permission from the author, except for the inclusion of brief quotations in a review.

Copyright © 1995 by Terri Horvath

Library of Congress Cataloging in Publication Data
Horvath, Terri
Spread the word: how to promote nonprofit groups with a network of speakers / Terri Horvath -- 1st Edition
p. cm.
Includes bibliographical references and index.
1. Sales promotion
2. Public relations
3. Public speaking
I. Title
HF5438.5H67 1995   658.8'2
                      QBI95-20218
ISBN 0-9644364-0-X: $14.95, softcover

Acknowledgments

Many thanks to those people who contributed their time and talents to help me present the information in this book. They include:

Pat Hatcher, who coordinates the Speakers Bureau roster for Kiwanis International
Stephen W. Duff, Public Affairs Coordinator for the Insurance Institute of Indiana
Marianne Downey, Director of Development for Catholic Social Services of Central Indiana
Beth Schmidt with the Assistance League of Indianapolis

proofreaders and editors
Beverly Smith, president of BKS Communications
Jerry Wilson of Jerry Wilson and Associates
Dorothy Smith and **Naomi Tropp** of The Julian Center
Suzanne Green Metzer of Corporate Masters
Pam Boggs of Boggs and Associates
Sharon Emmons

Dan Poynter who helped steer me in production and promotion

my husband **Dennis Horvath**

and friends **Bob and Mary Kraft, Frank and Nancy Bibbins and Boyd and Deanne Obermeyer**

Cover illustration by T/Maker and ClickArt

Table of Contents

About the Author	i
Introduction	ii-iv
Definition of a Speakers Bureau	v

Chapter One: Developing the bureau's structure and administration

Questions to answer	1-2
Answers result in three important decisions	1-3 & 4
Organizational tips	1-5, 6 & 9
Examples of standardized forms	1-7, 8, 10, 11, 12, 13, 14
Operational outline	1-15 & 16
Resources	1-17

Chapter Two: Working with the Speakers

Should you use staff, volunteers or both?	2-1 & 2
Developing your speakers' platform skills	2-2, 3 & 4
Recruiting volunteers	2-5, 6 & 7
Motivating your volunteers	2-7 & 8
Other sources for finding and training volunteers	2-10
Other tips	2-11
Resources	2-12

Chapter Three: Writing the Speech

The introduction, middle and end	3-1, 2 & 3
Other tips for writing and delivering the speech	3-4, 5, & 6
Things to avoid	3-7
Resources	3-8

Chapter Four: Publicizing the bureau

Before you send your first news release	4-1 & 2
Your basic PR tool	4-3, 4, 5, 6, 7, 8 & 9
Public Service Announcements	4-9 & 10
The next step	4-11, 12, 13 &14
Another viewpoint on marketing	4-15 & 16
There is intelligent life beyond the media	4-17 & 18
One more step	4-18
Resources	4-19

Afterword

5-1

Appendix A

Analysis of speech construction	A 1-5
Sample of canned speech	A 6-20

Appendix B

Summary of Resources   B 1-3

Index

C 1-2

About the Author

One of Terri Horvath's first jobs involved coordinating a speakers bureau for a nonprofit organization. Eighteen years later, she helped to establish a for-profit speakers bureau which caters to sales, business and technology groups needing speakers and trainers.

During those in-between years, Terri worked, and continues to do so, as a writer, photographer and desktop publisher. Her portfolio covers a variety of subjects from photographing and writing about the ballet to translating the process of wastewater treatment for the layman. Totaling over 1000 articles to her credit, Terri has written for both national and regional magazines as well as for companies and organizations in her hometown of Indianapolis, Indiana.

Her interest in photography has also encouraged her to explore the medium as an art form, and her photographs have been exhibited in several regional art shows.

Spread the Word: How to promote nonprofits with a network of speakers is her first book in a series she plans to devote to some of the specific needs of the not-for-profit industry.

Introduction

The Information Age has become cluttered. Thousands of publications have sprung up in recent years, and the not-for-profit organization's promotional materials must vie with its compatriots' for shrinking corporate, government and community funding. You need creative and distinctive ways to reach your marketplace, whether you manufacture a product, provide a service, or search for donations.

A network of speakers who promote your message is the verbal ingredient in your communication recipe. Mix this group, also known as a speakers bureau, with other public relations efforts, and your multifaceted creation can nourish even those who didn't know they were hungry for your message.

Establishing a speakers bureau for your organization can help spread the word about your goals and activities, increase community awareness, and build recognition of your organization as an authority in your field. As a ripple effect or even a direct consequence, a speakers bureau could facilitate convincing potential donors to contribute financial support. And the demand for speakers is plentiful.

The 1994 Meetings Outlook Survey, conducted by Meeting Professionals International and the American Society of Association Executives, indicates that the meeting industry continues to grow. Twenty-five percent of respondents say that they will hold more meetings in 1995, and 62 percent forecast that they will conduct at least the same number in 1996.

This trend extends to meetings that accommodate thousands of people or just a few; Fortune 500 companies and local community service clubs, schools, churches, and civic and professional groups.

People attend these meetings for a variety of reasons: fellowship, networking or just to take a break from their jobs. Perhaps the most valuable motive, however, is that the meeting is an efficient way to disburse information to several people at one time.

Another advantage to this type of communication format is emphasized in **Better Business Meetings**. Authors Robert B. Nelson and Peter Economy contend that the meeting allows for interaction, as opposed to a passive communicative form like a memo or newsletter. "If the recipient of the information is unclear about the intent or content of the information, you can resolve the issues in real time right then and there. Meetings allow for questions and answers and additional clarifications as needed. They allow for the next step or action to be taken as a result of a common understanding and discussion of the situation at hand."

Your speakers can fill this educational need while getting the word out about your organization.

This book outlines some of the details you should consider in establishing and operating a speakers bureau for your organization. The book has been divided into four major areas:

1. **Developing the bureau's structure and administration**
   The advantages of creating structure

Strategic questions to ask yourself about the purpose of the bureau and its administration
Tips from other bureau coordinators

2. **Working with the speakers**
   Deciding on the qualities you want in your speakers
   How to supplement your staff with volunteers
   How to determine the type of training you need for your speakers
   Recruiting and motivation tips

3. **Writing the speech**
   To "can" or not to "can
   Tips to generate audience interest

4. **Publicizing the bureau**
   Why developing a position statement is important before sending any material
   Tips for writing your basic PR tool—the news release
   Outlets besides newspapers, magazines, and broadcast media

Several examples of form letters, news releases and the text of speeches from various bureaus, also are included to amplify and clarify these four main sections. If you need additional information on any of these sections, you can refer to the listing of resources and publications at the end of each section.

The main purpose of this book is to provide guidelines to get your speakers bureau operational as an adjunct in your communication plans.

Your speakers bureau can create a human link between your organization and the community. In our sophisticated information age, the face-to-face approach still proves a valuable way to communicate.

85% of all new information will come through meetings--
Futurist Marvin Cetron

> For the purposes of this book, a speakers bureau is defined as a network of staff and/or volunteers who are knowledgeable about your organization and who will speak before an audience about specific issues or causes related to your organization.

Chapter One

Developing the bureau's structure and administration

To help ensure a successful venture, entrepreneurs develop a business plan or strategy for the company's progress. In this plan, the business owner also defines his/her product and how to market it. These points apply in establishing your speakers bureau.

In addition to a business plan, successful companies and organizations install some type of structure in the initial stages. This procedure also has four specific advantages for the bureau:

1. It eliminates the need to make the same decisions again and again. A structure allows you to pass along procedures and history to others easily.

2. It promotes trust. Everyone wants to know the extent of his/her responsibilities and those of others; you should provide a clear explanation of those expectations.

3. It provides a means for growth. You will find recruiting new members easier if everyone knows how the bureau operates.

4. It creates a system in which each person can participate fully. You encourage the speaker's growth and interest.

When planning your agency's speakers bureau, consider these questions:

- What excites you and other key personnel about your agency?

- What is the future for your agency?

- How can you incorporate this excitement and your goals in your speakers bureau?

- How can the speakers bureau and/or your agency help the community?

- Whom do you wish to reach? What is your target audience?

- How do you get the word out?

- Who will be involved?

- What skills do you seek in the speakers you select?

- Will you use volunteer speakers?

- What type of training do your speakers need?

- Should you schedule periodic meetings to keep your volunteers updated?

- What is your budget?

- Is your service free, or are you requesting a fee for your speakers? If you accept an honorarium, what are the tax considerations?

- What type of results do you expect? What is it you are trying to accomplish? What message do you want your bureau to relay?

- What is the primary reason for your bureau's existence? Do you want to seek contributions? Enlighten or educate the community? Seek new members for your group?

- What sets you apart from other nonprofit speakers bureaus?

- What means do you have for evaluating or measuring the milestones?

Your answers can provide the outline for your bureau. By undertaking this Q&A process, you decide on three important aspects of your bureau:

1. **the image and message you want to project.** A good example of an issues-oriented bureau is the one supported by the Insurance Institute of Indiana (III), an educational and lobbying group for several property/casualty insurance firms. III volunteers speak on a variety of topics concerning the property/casualty industry such as saving money on auto insurance or handling the results of an accident. III management determined that its bureau's mission is to help the general public better understand issues affecting their insurance needs.

All your bureau speakers should relay the same message. As individuals their opinions may vary slightly or even greatly, but when they are representing your organization, the speakers should present a united message. If they send conflicting messages to the public, they will undermine the overall mission of your bureau.

2. the audience you want to reach. In today's onslaught of communication efforts, people screen and reject much of the information offered. We want information that affects our lives or interests. This also applies to your efforts. You need to select the material that has the best chance of getting through to a specific audience. You must define your target market.

Who could benefit from the information you present? Whom do you want to reach, and why should they be interested? Are you looking for corporate sponsorships? Does your agency affect a specific segment of society, such as those concerned with children's welfare?

Reviewing the answers to these questions will help narrow your public relations efforts. Otherwise, you could spend a lot of money and still not reach those you seek.

In determining your target market, don't rely on one or two people's opinions. Ask your staff or key volunteers for input. Question friends who might know something about your group. Consider sending a short survey to members or contributors to determine their thoughts on the segment(s) of society you serve and should reach.

3. the best candidates to participate as speakers. If you are like many nonprofit groups, your department consists of the smallest number of staff needed to get the job done effectively-sometimes, not even that. This condition presents one of the best reasons for your agency to have a network of speakers:

volunteers help fill in the workday gaps. They provide backup when you cannot squeeze another moment out of your day to speak before an audience. However, their skills and knowledge may not match your objectives. Staff or volunteers? Training or not? Your decision depends upon the strategy you devise.

If you can find knowledgeable people with speaking experience, you have eliminated some of your initial work. (More information on recruiting speakers is available in the *Working with speakers* section.)

Now, if you merely skimmed the questions (on pages 1-2 & 3) for developing a business plan, go back, review them again. Devote some time and energy to answering them. By spending this time up front in the development of your bureau and your positioning statement, you'll save yourself time, money, and frustration in the long run.

More organizational tips

A speakers bureau, like any effort, can prove burdensome without structure and organization. Defining your objectives, your target market, and your network of speakers provides a skeletal foundation. To flesh out your organization, consider these tips:

- Gain the support of your agency's director or president. If he/she understands your efforts, he sets a tone of importance for the rest of the staff. The others will follow his lead.

- Determine who will serve as coordinator. Stephen Duff, of the Insurance of Institute of Indiana, recommends appointing one coordinator to avoid confusion and duplicate efforts.

- Design standardized forms. For example, standardized confirmation letters and printed checklists save time and confusion in finalizing the arrangements between the speaker and the group to be addressed. (See checklist on page 1-7.)

- Think about any support staff you need. Do you need extra clerical help? Once again, look to your volunteers for additional assistance.

- Ask questions of the contact requesting a speaker to determine his and the group's expectations. Listening carefully to his response will save embarrassing oversights and miscommunications.

- Send a confirmation letter to both the person making the request and the speaker. Confirm all the pertinent information so that neither misunderstands the expectations. (See sample 1 on page 1-11. For the sake of legibility, the original form was not copied. However, the items on the form are listed as intended.)

- Provide a one-page synopsis to the contact of the speech or topic to be presented. (See the chapter on publicity for more details)

- Log all speaking engagements. Keeping track of who speaks and what organizations make the request can prove valuable. For example, Duff does not like to overburden any one individual with too many requests. Duff's log helps him spread out assignments   *--see 1-9*

Checklist for Presentation

- [ ] Determined size of audience
- [ ] Determined location, with directions
- [ ] Have a written introduction of speaker
- [ ] Have a microphone (if needed)
- [ ] Have notes, speech, and/or outline
- [ ] Podium/lectern provided
- [ ] Have visual aids ready including flip chart
- [ ] Have all equipment needs arranged
- [ ] Have emergency backup equipment, such as extra extension cords or projector bulbs.
- [ ] Confirmed time of arrival and subject of speech

You also will need to provide introductory information on the speaker and your organization and determine if a biography of the speaker should be sent in advance. Ask which group will do the publicity and if a stage and microphone are provided, which may be necessary for large groups. In addition, determine if the group will want a Q&A session.

Other items you may want to check off include the following items that may assist the speaker or group:

☐ A/V needs

☐ Blackboard or easel

☐ Photo of speaker for publicity

☐ Fact sheet of your organization sent

☐ Video

☐ Pointer

- among all the speakers. Maintaining a list of those making the requests can also help in your marketing efforts next year: you know who needs speakers. Keeping a file on the type of requests also is important to determine the relevance of topic. For Duff, who has several canned presentations, his records help him evaluate which topics should be kept and which should be discarded.

- Respond quickly to requests for information. In this fax-mentality age, people want answers more quickly than ever, and they want to know someone is there. For those without secretaries or receptionists, providing access to voice mail may prove the answer. Return calls as soon as possible--at least within 24 hours.

- Obtain feedback from the groups requesting speeches. Ask your contact to complete an evaluation form on each speaker. (See samples 2a and 2b on pages 1-12 & 13. Originals not copied.) You also should make a follow-up call after the speech to the initial contact. This is another way to show that the bureau is interested in the presentation effect and benefit for the audience. This follow-up information can help you improve the bureau and provide ideas for new topics.

- Request that your speaker submit a brief report following the presentation. (See sample 3 on page 1-14.)

Summary: Determine your message and who should hear it first. This initial effort makes bringing the two together much easier. Organizing and designing necessary checklists could prove almost as beneficial as the leading headache remedies.

When communicating with an organization requesting speakers, you will need the following information:

- topic requested

- date

- time of speech and length
  (a general guideline is 20-30 minutes)

- time speaker should arrive

- location and directions

- organization

- whom to meet upon speaker's arrival

- other speakers on program, if any, and their subjects

- size of audience

- size of room

Sample 1

Speakers & Seminar Resources, Inc.
Engagement Reminder

Today's Date:

To: *(contact's name)*

Dear *(contact's name):*
Just a reminder of the agreement for upcoming engagement of *(your organization's name)* speaker *(speaker's name):*

Date of engagement:

Location:

Time of presentation:
(and time that speaker needs to appear)

Fees and expenses: *(if applicable)*

Special Arrangements:
(include anything that the organization is to provide)

Please let me know if I can be of further assistance.

Sincerely,
(Your name)

***After the presentation, would you please complete the enclosed Presentation Evaluation and return it in the self-addressed, stamped envelope?

Sample 2a

**Speakers & Seminar Resources, Inc.
Presentation Evaluation**

Organization:
Contact Person:
Event Date:
Speaker:
Thank you for giving Speakers & Seminar Resources the opportunity to work with you on this event. Your feedback is very important, therefore, we would appreciate your input in evaluating the speaker. Your comments help us and the speaker to continuously improve our services.

                              Excellent Good Fair Poor
The presentation was_____
Information learned_____
Content related to topic_____
Audience response_____
Satisfied audience needs_____
Satisfied your needs_____
Service of the speaker_____

Would you recommend this speaker to others?_____
May we release your comments?_____
What are the best qualities about the speaker and/or the presentation?
What do you feel the speaker might alter or improve for future presentations?
What recommendations can you give that would enhance our service to you?
(The original form does provide space for answers.)

Sample 2b

Insurance Institute of Indiana
Speakers Bureau
SPEAKER EVALUATION FORM

Date:
Location:
Group:
Topic:
Speaker's Name:

1. Was the speaker's topic useful/enjoyable?
    Yes_____ No_____
Comments:

2. Could the presentation be heard clearly?
    Yes_____ No_____

3. Did the speaker do anything to distract from what he/she was presenting?
    Yes_____ No_____

If yes, what?

4. Did the speaker stay focused on the topic that he/she was presenting? Yes_____ No_____

5. Are there any suggestions you could offer that would make the speaker's presentation better?

6. Please list any other insurance speakers and/or topics that you would like to hear.
(The original form does provide space for answers.)

Sample 3

Items for Speaker's Evaluation

- Date of presentation

- Group name

- Size of audience

- Audience's reaction

- Types of questions asked

- Questions that the speaker could not answer

- Any problems in the topic/speech, communication with bureau or expectation of audience

- Other comments

(III hands out the following information to all speakers in its bureau.)

Insurance Institute of Indiana
Speakers Bureau

Operation

1. The chief executive officer of each member company identifies volunteers from the organization who are willing to deliver presentations on behalf of the Institute. Usually, these people are in middle to upper management, with broad training and experience in the insurance industry. Of course, oral communication skills are also of great importance.

2. Each volunteer participating in the speakers bureau is asked to complete a biographical information form which will be used to develop a script for his/her introduction at speeches.

3. Institute staff promotes the speakers bureau and elicits requests for speeches. Mailings with speaker request forms will be sent to major civic groups and agent organizations throughout Indiana and the bureau will be advertised in several insurance industry publications including the Indiana Underwriter and the Independent Insurance Agents of Indiana newsletter.

4. Participants in the Employee Education Program will also be asked to find one to two venues per month at which the Institute can schedule speeches. These speeches will be set up through the so that the speeches can be rotated throughout the participants.

5. When requests are received in the Institute office, the Public Affairs Coordinator contacts a volunteer speaker at one of the participating companies.

6. The Institute will contact the participating companies on a rotating basis to assure that no company is unfairly burdened.

7. After the speaker has been identified and the information relayed to the Institute, a confirmation letter to the speaker, as well as to the person who initially requested the presentation, will be sent. This would include all the details, time, place, topic, size of audience, etc. plus biographical information which may be used as an introduction for the speaker.

8. Speakers are provided with speeches for each topic as well as a detailed outline, but speakers are encouraged not to read the text, but rather use it as a guide for developing their own, personalized remarks. Speakers will also be given copies of an appropriate brochure for each topic to hand out at each speech.

9. The Institute will follow up the speech with a written evaluation form.

Resources

How to Write a Successful Business Plan, by Julie Brooks and Barry A. Stevens (New York, NY, American Management Association, 1987).

Positioning: The Battle for Your Mind, by Al Ries and Jack Trout (New York, NY, McGrawHill, 1981).

Getting Started on Strategic Planning, by John M. Bryson in cassette form (San Francisco, CA, JosseyBass, Inc., 1991).

Doing Well While Doing Good: The Marketing Link Between Business & Nonprofit Causes, by Lawrence L. Embley (Englewood Cliffs, NJ, Prentice Hall, 1993).

You Are the Message: Secrets of Master Communicators, by Roger Ailes with Jon Kraushar (New York, NY, Doubleday, 1989).

Chapter Two

Working with the Speakers

Staff or volunteers?

Supplementing your staff with knowledgeable volunteers can be a time-saving, stress reducer. Your volunteer speakers can ease the work load. Depending on the breadth and depth of your bureau's efforts, your presentations may require more time than you imagine. You spend much more than the 20 or 30 minutes allotted for a speech. You also have to calculate the time needed for preparation, driving to the location, probably eating lunch or dinner, discussion afterward, driving back, and any necessary follow-up. All this can easily consume a half-day or even more. Multiply that time by the number of speeches, and you and your staff can accumulate more hours than initially envisioned.

Adding volunteers to your bureau also can help you extend your reach into the community through their own connections. And the involvement makes volunteers feel a part of the organization. You also will be able to meet multiple demands. If one organization asks for a speaker on the same day as another, you then have several options to accommodate both groups.

However, the concerns and issues your bureau addresses may require more in-depth knowledge than most laypersons possess.

The main advantage of using staff members only is that they know (or should know) their field of expertise and the agency in greater detail. If you use volunteer speakers, you will need to provide sufficient education on the issues and platform training. Don't underestimate the need for your speaker to be well-trained and informed. An unprepared speaker does not add to your organization's good reputation.

When the speakers feel well-informed, they project confidence and commitment. Allow them time to practice their speeches with the staff before sending them out to face an audience. Direct some typical questions that might arise and help them formulate answers. If they don't know the answers, don't encourage them to bluff responses, but provide a means to follow-up after their presentations with replies.

> **Here's another tip:**
>
> The League of Women Voters of the United States lists three tips for finding the neophyte suitable for your bureau:
> 1. They should be interesting.
> 2. They should be easy to understand.
> 3. They should be comfortable before an audience.

Developing your speakers' platform skills

Now you need to decide if you prefer experienced speakers, staffers, dedicated volunteers, or any combination of the three. Finding experienced presenters will make your job easier, because they usually have good verbal communication skills. Are they as eager, however, to devote time to learning about your organization? Knowing the field is as important as speaking well.

Turning to dedicated volunteers, who already have devoted hours to your agency and to increasing their own understanding of your cause, presents a viable alternative. But you must ask: Are they competent speakers? And you will find that the idea of speaking in public terrifies most people. (Public speaking has been documented as the number one fear of the general population, ranking well above the fear of death.) Motivating those dedicated volunteers into podium-action, therefore, can be challenging.

In order to get the ideal speaker, you will need to provide some raining--knowledge in your agency and causes for the experienced speaker and platform skills for the novice presenter. The Insurance Institute of Indiana, for example, sponsors a half-day workshop for volunteer speakers. Coordinator Stephen Duff explains the material and brings in a trainer to help volunteers polish their presentation skills.

Once you have identified those people who could serve as speakers, you must build their confidence. Here are some recommendations that the speakers can use to help build their courage:

- Remember the overall message. When you focus on what you say instead of how you say it, you will feel your comfort level rise.

- Relate a relevant story that interests you. Storytellers throughout the ages have discovered that a good story builds a rapport that few other devices can duplicate. The connection is a shared feeling that helps the speaker feel that he/she is speaking with the audience, not at or to them.

- Visualize yourself succeeding before the group. These visualization techniques help to put your stomach's butterflies in proper flying formation.

- Be yourself, and your sincerity will show through. Perhaps the greatest tranquilizer for the nerves is knowing that most audiences want you to succeed. They want to be entertained and educated. Generally you really do have a room full of supporters whenever and wherever you speak.

- Remember your sense of humor. Victor Borge once said that the shortest distance between two people is laughter. But more than establishing rapport, laughing affects you physically as well. When you laugh you take in oxygen which improves your circulation and reduces stress. A word of caution: People's senses of humor vary dramatically, so use yours with care. Consider your audience once again, and look to jokes or anecdotes that prove nonoffensive. Before trying any joke on an audience, test it on friends or colleagues. Perhaps the safest recourse lies in using your wit and a sincere smile instead. You may not get the belly laughs that you could with a good joke, but you project a likable and enjoyable presence.

"Courage comes from wanting to say it well.
Security comes from knowing you can say it well.
Confidence comes from having said it well."
Sharon Anthony Bower in **Painless Public Speaking**

Recruiting volunteers

In the ideal situation, volunteers thunder forth, eager in their opportunity to help your cause. Lucky you, if you have such a group. Most bureau coordinators, however, will have to conduct some kind of recruiting effort.

A general announcement in your newsletter or at a meeting may draw some volunteers. If that fails, take the personal approach. Ask specific members or other volunteers who have shown speaking ability or demonstrated their commitment to become part of your speakers bureau. And if that doesn't work, consider some other sources:

- Ask for recommendations. If the current volunteer isn't interested, perhaps he/she knows a friend or coworker who is.

- Get the word out. Once your bureau is in operation, allow your speakers to share volunteer opportunities within your organization including involvement in the speakers bureau.

- Collaborate efforts with another like-minded organization and combine both agencies' resources, including a list of volunteer speakers. An example is found in the United Way's annual fund campaign. The United Way of Indianapolis will send a speaker from one of the agencies it supports to a corporation or club to talk about that agency's work and how it depends on the contributions made to the United Way. There may be similar examples in your community.

- Contact your local Volunteer Action Center. Although the names may vary, these offices exist across the country and in Canada. Their common mission is to help other organizations recruit and refer volunteers. Some also provide leadership and management training and host resource libraries on issues of interest to nonprofit groups.

- Call on colleges and other educational institutions as well as groups like Toastmasters. Organizations like these can direct you to people specifically wanting this type of opportunity to improve their speaking skills or add depth to their resumes.

- Contact local companies, industries or government agencies that may want to help in your efforts. Do you have a major corporate contributor or supporter which may have a cadre of potential volunteer speakers?

- Be ready to sign up volunteers in any circumstances. When you are outside your office, have plenty of brochures and a sign-up sheet available. Be sure to get the

---

In **Secrets of Motivation: How to Get and Keep Volunteers and Paid Staff!**, author Sue Vineyard shares her most important tip: "We must understand and accept people where they are, then work to let them know where we are going, why, and how they can help in our journey toward the vision of a better tomorrow. We must find ways to work with them as they join our journey and appreciate their efforts and resources for as long as they contribute."

interested prospect's phone number, and followup with that person quickly.

Motivating your volunteers

Ray Francis studied volunteers' motivation for his thesis at the University of Wisconsin and discovered that when volunteers are given a job that matches their personal motivations, three things happen:
1. They accept the positions more readily.
2. They have greater satisfaction.
3. They stay longer.

In addition, they place a high value on education as an outcome of their volunteerism. If they learn from the experience, they are more likely to respond positively. Improving their communication skills by giving speeches for your organization, therefore, works to your advantage. One of the greatest skills needed today to successfully compete in the marketplace is good communication. You can help volunteers improve those skills.

To keep their good faith, however, you must keep them well-informed and provide some type of training. People want to feel part of the team, and this free flow of information helps them feel that way.

Stephen Duff, of The Insurance Institute of Indiana, adds that it also is important to spread the assignments around. Involve all your volunteers as frequently as possible. Even though some may prove more effective than others, you want to keep a healthy supply of volunteers available. Keeping them active also maintains their interest and motivation.

Expressing your appreciation also is a key factor in motivating volunteers. For example, the Insurance Institute of Indiana holds a dinner for its speakers and presents an award for the one giving the most speeches during the year.

Yet what seems like an honor to one may be insignificant to another. Or you may not be able financially to host an affair like a dinner. You may have to seek other means to express your appreciation that match the individual's interests or goals and your budget.

Other ways to recognize your volunteers could include the following:

1. Send thank-you notes to volunteers, their bosses, and/or their families.

2. Write articles about their participation.

3. Ask them for advice and ways to improve the bureau.

4. Nominate one or more for community awards.

5. Present them with personalized mementos, such as certificates, coffee cups or T-shirts.

6. Offer leads to help in their jobs or businesses.

7. Increase their responsibility.

8. Increase their exposure to the community.

Summary: Desire, preparation, practice and commitment. Initially, volunteers are attracted by their vision of your organization or by their own unique means to make a contribution. When you present the vision and how they can help make it a reality, you lay the foundation for your volunteers' motivation. Empower them with your vision and with proper training. Recognize their efforts in small and large ways. Sometimes all it takes is a "thank-you" in front of peers for a job well-done.

Committed volunteers are like extra staff members for your speakers bureau, and they don't expect much money. They can prove a valuable asset, particularly for the one-person office coordinating a speakers bureau.

Other sources for finding and training volunteers:

Toastmasters International has an extensive network of chapters. Members develop and practice their presentation skills on a regular basis. Your local chamber of commerce or library may be able to refer you to the nearest chapter. Toastmasters International's address is P.O. Box 9052, Mission Viejo, CA 92690. 714-858-8255.

Your local Volunteer Action Center (which may be known under a slightly different name) should be listed in the telephone directory. If you have difficulty locating it, ask the nearest United Way office. Many centers are affiliated with the local UW. If not, the staff probably will know how you can reach the center.

The Indiana University Center on Philanthropy provides literature and workshops on volunteerism. The address is 550 W. North Street, Suite 301, Indianapolis, IN 46202-3162. 317-274-4200.

According to Frederick Herzbergis in his Motivational-Hygiene Theory, people are motivated by the following five factors:
1. achievement
2. recognition
3. challenging work
4. increased responsibility
5. growth and development

General tips on preparing visual aids:

- Don't cram too much information onto a single slide or overhead.

- Use large type in your slides, so that those seated in the back of room can also see. If colors are used, be sure they are not competing and confusing.

- Eliminate as much extraneous light as possible when using slides.

- Try not to mix the types of visual aids you use, going from flip chart to overhead to slides and then video.

- Remember the advice of Frank Paolo, author of **How to Make a Great Presentation in 2 Hours**: "Some of the best visual aids are the simplest because they demand that audience members interact with your presentation. The best way for audience members to interact is taking notes from an outlined structure." On this outline, he suggests you provide plenty of white space for the audience to write 1. your (the speaker or agency's) objective 2. two or three key points you want them to remember and 3. possibly your title.

Resources

Painless Public Speaking, by Sharon Anthony Bower (Englewood Cliffs, NJ, Prentice Hall, 1981).

Secrets of Motivation: How to Get & Keep Volunteers & Paid Staff!, by Sue Vineyard (Downers Grove, IL, Heritage Arts, 1991).

Recruiting Volunteers: A Guide for Non-Profits, by Mary Ann Burke and Carl Liljenstolpe (Los Altos, CA, Crisp Publications, 1992).

Leadership and Management of Volunteer Programs, by James C. Fisher (San Francisco, CA, Jossey-Bass, Inc., 1993).

Speak and Grow Rich, by Dottie Walters and Lilly Walters (Englewood Cliffs, NJ, Prentice Hall, 1989).

Megatrends and Volunteerism, by Sue Vineyard, (Downers Grove, IL, Heritage Arts Publishing, a division of VMSystems, 1993).

101 Tips for Volunteer Recruitment, by Steve MCurley and Sue Vineyard, (Downers Grove, IL, Heritage Arts Publishing, 1988).

Still More Games Trainers Play, by Edward E. Scannell and John W. Newstrom, (New York, NY, McGraw-Hill, 1991).

Chapter Three

Writing the Speech

If you study those speeches that have truly affected people (such as Martin Luther King's "I Have a Dream"), you discover the reason for their memorable aspects. The writer composed his thoughts and words to affect the ear, mind, and heart. The ideal speech includes a cadence and rhythm to grab people's attention, material to stimulate the intellect without clutter, and emotional content to bind the presenter and his listener. Yet a presentation that can do all that is rare. If you think that you already can accomplish those aspects, you don't need to read this section. Most of us, however, are journeymen working toward these goals.

This chapter examines some key elements and tips in writing speeches and their delivery. You may want your volunteers to write their own, or perhaps you prefer compiling the material yourself.

Whether they write the speech or use yours, you want them to talk like themselves, which helps them exude confidence. But you know there are pertinent facts to be covered as well. Therefore, you may want to write the material for them. Many bureau coordinators do prepare a "canned" speech (see Appendix A), which gives the volunteer speakers a format to follow

with all the pertinent data. The reasoning for this canned text is three-fold:
1. to provide a basic format,
2. to cover the key elements and pertinent facts, and
3. to ensure consistent delivery of the material.

Bureau coordinators also know that a speech that is read becomes monotonous; therefore, they also provide an outline of the key points, which allows the speaker some flexibility while still covering the pertinent issues.

Whether you or a volunteer undertakes the writing responsibilities, the first task is to determine the purpose of the speech. Is it to inform, motivate, persuade, or a combination of these? The answer clarifies your goals and facilitates preparing an outline. You know where you're heading. Some writers recommend writing the beginning and the end at the same time, before proceeding to the middle. This exercise helps focus on the expected outcome.

Consider also allowing the speaker to open with a personal story relevant to your agency and his/her interest in its cause. Throughout history, storytelling has proven itself as a connecting tool between the teller and the audience. A good story helps to establish rapport. Perhaps the speaker could explain why he/she is interested in your organization. When the audience sees that the speaker cares about the subject, which a story tends to project, then the people relate.

In writing the speech, remember that there is a purpose to each of the three parts of the material.

- **The introduction,** such as the speaker's own story, gets the attention of the audience. It makes the audience feel a connection--they understand the relevance of what's to come for their own situation. This beginning also announces the central thought or statement of the speech and can consist of one or several paragraphs. Your audience wants to feel involved. What's in it for them? Tell them why they should feel the connection, and get to the point as early as possible. Studies show that putting an important idea at the beginning increases retention by as much as 75 percent.

- **The middle** presents any facts, anecdotes, and/or reasoning that make the central thought understandable. This provides the substance to the purpose of the speech, and, of course, constitutes the bulk of the material.

- **The end** alerts the audience that the speech is concluding and serves as a bridge from the main body. The end also can appeal to the audience's needs, repeat the central thought, summarize the main point, and/or call for a plan of action. In addition, just as you want to grab the audience at the beginning, you want to leave them with a memorable final statement. The

---

Speech openers that can get an audience's attention quickly:
- a compliment
- questions/rhetorical questions
- a startling statement or statistic
- a joke
- a visual aid
- a reference to a current event
- a quotation
- a story

result should be some type of reaction. To help in this, the speaker should maintain eye contact throughout the ending. Encourage your speakers to memorize the ending, and avoid reading the text.

Other tips for writing and delivering the speech:

- Use visual aids to help illustrate point, but don't rely on aids to make the point alone.

- If you plan to use audio-visual equipment, have hard copies of the messages as back-up. Even if you plan for a breakdown of equipment, and have back-up gear, the unthinkable sometimes occurs, and your back-up gear fails.

- Beware of jargon. You may know what you're talking about, but your objective is to make sure the audience does, too. Choose a vocabulary suitable for the audience. This includes clarifying abbreviations and acronyms.

- Use appropriate humor. Humor, like storytelling, helps grab your audience and increases their retention of the material. However, don't use jokes that might offend a segment of society.

- Prefix an important point with a flag such as "This is vital," or "Listen to this." This helps to increase the audience's memory up to 90 percent.

- Repeat an important segment to help spur the audience's recall.

- Avoid name-dropping. It's a turn-off.

- Involve the audience whenever possible. Asking questions, playing games, or inviting their opinions are a few suggestions for audience involvement.

- Double-check your facts. Never assume that one source is always right without substantial credentials.

- Stay within the allotted time frame.

- Allow time for questions.

- Generate at least one question to help lead the Q&A period. Often people are shy about starting; having one example provides incentive. You can either have the speaker present the question from the platform or ask one of the audience members to do the honors.

    You may get a few hostile questions. To help diffuse the resulting tension, remind your speakers to focus on the

---

The speech should appeal to the auditory, kinesthetic, and visual ways in which we learn. Each individual learns in a different way and, therefore, each method demands an element that grab his/her interest.

For those who relate on the auditory level, a good introductory story may stimulate their interest. Kinesthetic learners, those who learn by touching or doing, may relate to such tools as handout materials or some type of written or physical exercise. To establish a visual rapport, you may need slides, overhead transparencies, or similar aids.

facts of the issue, not the emotions. Suggest they keep a cool head, answer the question with facts and understanding, and then move on to other questions from the audience.

- Do not encourage your speakers to bluff an answer. If they don't know the answer, tell them to encourage the audience member to contact the bureau coordinator or the appropriate agency representative. Or the speaker may want to find the answer and contact the questioner afterward.

- Review the information in each speech periodically, and update the information if necessary.

- Never speak more than 60 seconds after saying "In conclusion."

Summary: Determine the purpose of your speech. Understanding your objective--whether it's to inform, motivate, or persuade--will help clarify your writing efforts.

Here's another tip

In the first 30 seconds, the speaker is either received or rejected by the audience. This initial impression is determined:
- 88% by sight
- 7% by hearing
- 3.5% by smell
- 1.5% by touch

What your audience *sees* is vital.

Things to Avoid

The 10 most common problems in communications, as listed by Roger Ailes in **You Are the Message: Secrets of the Master Communicators:**

1. Lack of initial rapport with listeners

2. Stiffness or woodenness in use of body

3. Presentation of material is intellectually oriented, forgetting to involve the audience emotionally

4. Speaker seems uncomfortable because of fear of failure

5. Poor use of eye contact and facial expression

6. Lack of humor

7. Speech direction and intent unclear, due to improper preparation

8. Inability to use silence for impact

9. Lack of energy, causing inappropriate pitch pattern, speech rate and volume

10. Use of boring language and a lack of interesting material

Resources

The Public Speakers Bible, by Stuart Turner (Wellinborough, Thorsons Publishing Group, 1988).

The Art of Plain Talk, by Rudolf Flesch (New York, NY, Harper & Brothers, 1946).

The Quick and Easy Way to Effective Speaking, by Dale Carnegie (New York, NY, Pocket Books, 1977).

Instant Eloquence: a lazy man's guide to public speaking, by James C. Humes (New York, NY, Harper & Row, 1973).

Roles Speakers Play, by James C. Humes (New York, NY, Harper & Row, 1976).

Chapter Four

Publicizing the bureau

Most bureau coordinators know that publicity is essential to the bureau's use. Pat Hatcher, who coordinates the Kiwanis International Speakers Bureau, notes that the volume of requests correspond directly to the amount of publicity conducted in the preceding weeks.

The frequency of your mailings will depend upon your needs. Should you target a mailing immediately before a big fund drive? Is there a better time? Or do you prefer to send information out on a periodic basis? As an example, Insurance Institute sends a release to all outlets in Indiana only once a year. Other organizations may want to publicize the bureau quarterly or monthly. The amount of exposure, through the news media or other sources, directly affects the number of speaking engagements.

Before you send your first news release

Most bureau coordinators agree that getting the word out is the most difficult aspect of their job. They look for publicity sources that are cost-efficient (meaning as cheaply as possible). Yet the media does not always have the same agenda. Publicity is essential, but it comes in many forms and does not always have to involve the media. Is there one easy way? Probably not. Work is involved, and it takes time. But when you have set a clearly defined goal and market, you have taken the first step.

The positioning statement you developed earlier will help you decide where to concentrate your PR efforts. Whether you have a large or small budget, marketing experts recommend taking the "rifle" approach, which refers to trying to reach a well-defined market or niche. Determine a specific market, and learn which media reach them. Plan your PR around this market primarily. If you blanket the general population with releases, your efforts become diffused and financially inefficient. This doesn't mean you shouldn't include those outside your target market if they should hear about your speakers bureau; but focus your publicity efforts in specific areas.

Does your target market have its own trade magazine or newsletter? The insurance industry in each state, for example, usually has its own publications tailored to its interests. If your market primarily is directed toward women, look for a specific outlet that influences them, like a regional women's magazine. Or your market could be the local bar association, CPA society, association executives' organization, Junior League, and so on, all of which probably have newsletters.

Think about how to reach these people in your defined markets. What do they read? Where do they live? What groups do they belong to? What are their churches or social activities? These are just some of the demographics you should examine. Refer back to the section on structure, and don't underestimate the need to define your market and your objectives before spending money on postage and news releases.

Your basic PR tool

Call it a news or media release, but don't call it a press release. People in the electronic media tend to take offense. This one- or two-page synopsis is the basic tool in getting your message out. (See sample 5 on 4-4.)

Your job in writing the release is to show an editor why your information will be of interest to his/her readers or listeners. Hundreds of releases cross an editor's desk every week.

What will make yours stand out and avoid getting your message buried?

Why would your target market want to read or hear about your organization? What's unique about your organization, and why is your speakers bureau important? Has an event happened recently that highlights your message? Has a specific publication or TV program covered an issue that affects your agency? Spell it out for the reporter or editor. They are busy people, and you need to grab their attention.

Suggested format and tips for the news release

The primary objectives of your news release are
1. to get it printed or aired,
2. to be noticed by the public.

The following lists several key points to include in a news release for the editor's convenience and to spark his/her interest:

Sample 5 (Put news release on your letterhead.)

Date:
Contact Person: Jane Doe
Phone: 555-555-5555

For immediate release

Facing the current state of uncertainty in the health care industry, XYZ Health Agency experts seek to help consumers understand their current options and future possibilities.

The agency recently established a speakers bureau composed of volunteers knowledgeable on health care-related issues.

These speakers are available, free of charge, for presentations on a variety of subjects. Topics include:

- How the proposed changes in our health care system affect the elderly.

- Can baby boomers afford to retire?

- How volunteerism affects the health care system.

  and more.

For more information on XYZ's bureau, call 555-555-5555.

###

Words that help sell the media on your release

advice	new
announces	novel
discovery	now
exclusive	only
expert	popular
first	prominent
future	proven
growth	recent
help--helpful	recommended
how to	respected
knowledgeable	scientific
latest	success
necessary	tested

- Include the release date which tells editors when they can print the information. Usually "For immediate release" is sufficient.

- Indicate your agency's contact person, address, phone, and fax number. If the editors have questions for an in-depth story, tell them who can give additional details.

- Suggest a headline for the article. Besides proving helpful to the editor, the headline serves as a means to encapsulate the text's main point.

- Open with a strong lead or statement to grab a reader's attention. The trend in feature writing today is to include a story about a person affected by an issue. For example, the release for an agency dealing with substance abuse might include a success story about someone who overcame an addiction and how the agency helped.

  The following lists some other attention grabbers. (Examples used are not necessarily true.)

  Incorporate the latest trend with your news.
  (Example: Low-fat snacks aid in back-injury recovery say chiropractors.)

  Challenge recent events.
  (Example: Insurance experts prove that latest federal statistics on auto insurance are inaccurate.)

  Provide a new slant on an old subject.
  (Example: Fitness guru says too much exercise is bad for your health.)

Make off-the-wall comparisons that actually do relate to your agency
(Example: Insects help clean office environments, according to property managers who have enlisted the aid of these tiny crusaders.)

- Remember the five W's and H--who, what, when, where, why and how. Which of these questions should receive top priority? Their answers should be as close to the top of your release as possible. (Articles usually are cut from the bottom up when space dictates such action.) The main purpose of your release is to announce that your speakers bureau is operating, and that knowledgeable volunteers are available to speak on a relevant subject.

- Use short sentences, action verbs, and short paragraphs as much as possible.

- Send the release to the right person. Who makes the decision about what is printed or broadcast?

- Be objective. Don't hype your efforts or become flowery with your praise.

- Include good quotes from your speeches or other sources. A good quote helps add interest.

- Keep it short, no more than one or two double-spaced pages. The double-spaced format allows editors to make additions or corrections easily and neatly.

- Use your letterhead or photocopies of the release on letterhead. Don't get cute with the paper, like using fluorescent orange to make it stand out. It's annoying.

- Include information about your speakers bureau on all of your news releases, even if the subject does not relate to the bureau. You never know how much space an editor may need to fill and when he/she might include all of the release. (A general rule, however, is to not exceed two pages.)

- Be persistent. Editors don't always keep releases on file. If they don't publish your release within an allotted time frame, send it to them again.

- End your release with the symbol ###, which is a standardized notation indicating "the end."

Why news releases are rejected.

The Lock Haven Express, a newspaper in Lock Haven, Pennsylvania, once compiled a list of reasons that releases sent to them failed to appear in the paper. Rejected releases had all or some of the following characteristics:
1. no local angle
2. lack of timeliness
3. poor news writing
4. too lengthy
5. too commercial
6 geared to influence editors rather than provide material for news.

- Include a photograph (acceptable standard is 5"x7", black & white) with the release if the photo adds interest and follows the publication's usual format.

Go beyond the fact that your speakers bureau exists. Tell the public why it exists.

PSAs

A Public Service Announcement (or PSA) is the verbal equivalent of the news release for radio and TV stations. These PSAs last up from 10 to 60 seconds.

Keep each PSA to one page, capitalize all letters, and triple-space the information. This helps the announcer organize and read the information. (See sample 6 on page 4-10.)

Although the PSA used to be a standard addition to PR professional's arsenal of publicity tools, today's stations limit these announcements. Save some money by sending these PSAs only to stations you know will run them.

Sample 6

FOR MORE INFORMATION: JANE DOE
555-555-5555

PUBLIC SERVICE ANNOUNCEMENT -- 10 SECONDS

FOR IMMEDIATE RELEASE

THE XYZ HEALTH AGENCY HAS FORMED A SPEAKERS BUREAU TO ANSWER CONSUMERS' QUESTIONS ABOUT THE COUNTRY'S HEALTH CARE SYSTEM. FOR MORE INFORMATION, CALL THE XYZ AGENCY, 555-555-5555.

The next step

Your budget may dictate the extent of your publicity efforts. You may want to forward as much information as possible in the first mailing, or keep it to the bare essentials. In either case, you should have certain items on file in case a reporter contacts you for more details.

In addition to the news release, the items for the complete media kit include:

- Photos. Keep photos of your speaker in action, head shots of your volunteer speakers or prominent staff members, and illustrations that show your agency in action. If you don't have a photo file, be willing to arrange quickly a photo shoot with the publication's or station's photographer.

- A fact sheet. This is a concise listing of pertinent facts about your agency. The fact sheet could include historical data, your mission statement, and other details. You might also create a list summarizing the topic of each speech.

- Biographical data of people involved in the speakers bureau. If they are well-known in the community, include this in your news release and fact sheets.

- Text of the speech. This helps the reporter prepare his questions and slant of the article.

- Agency brochure, if available. Your promotional material does not have to be elaborate. In fact, a simple, easy-to-read brochure may be the best approach. A slick, four-color brochure is nice and eye-catching, but not necessary. Remember, we're inundated with information from all kinds of sources, and reading it all proves difficult. Often it is preferable just to see all pertinent information in an organized, concise format. Even if you work with only copier paper, simple can be better. But with the advantages presented through the technology in desktop publishing, you could write and design effective material for minimal cost. (See sample 7 on pages 4-13 & 14.)

- A list of sample questions for radio and TV interviewers. Reporters may not use your suggestions, but the list will help if they don't have time to do adequate preparation. Plus, it gives you the chance to engineer the direction of the interview.

You can send your press release to one or all of these media contacts:

At the newspapers or magazines: city editor, section editors, individual reporters who have covered similar issues.

At radio stations: news directors, reporters, senior producers, assistant news directors, program directors.

At television stations: assignment editors, planning editors, reporters, news directors.

Once you have established rapport with reporters, keep them updated. Know their deadlines, their personalities, and the types of stories that interest them. Don't waste their time with information that does not suit their needs.

Sample 7

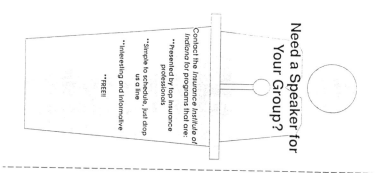

Need a Speaker for Your Group?

Contact the *Insurance Institute of Indiana* for programs that are:

* Presented by top insurance professionals
* Simple to schedule, just drop us a line
* Interesting and informative
* FREE!!

For interesting speakers programs: contact the Insurance Institute of Indiana Speakers Bureau.

Insurance Institute of Indiana
10 West Market Street
1120 Market Tower
Indianapolis, Ind. 46204

Insurance Institute of Indiana, Inc.
10 West Market Street
1120 Market Tower
Indianapolis, IN 46204-2964

Place Stamp Here

HOW TO RESERVE A SPEAKER

It is simple. Complete this request card, specifying the speech topic you would like to have presented to your group. Then just stamp and mail it to the Institute. We will send you a confirmation letter which includes the speaker's name and biographical information that can be used for his/her introduction at your meeting. Presentations are available at **no cost**.

Please send the request card at least four weeks in advance of your meeting date!

If you need more than one request card copy the attached one and place it in an envelope or call the Insurance Institute for additional cards.

Sample 7 continued

Does your group need a speaker or program?

Take a look at these!

How to Save Money on Your Auto Insurance

Many people complain about the cost of auto insurance. This program presents an outline of how insurance rates are set, how auto insurance works, and how people can save money on their auto insurance premiums.

How to Save Money on Insuring Your Home

This presentation explains simple things that can be done to save money on your homeowners insurance. It also examines how homeowners insurance functions and how to know how much to purchase for your own needs.

What Should Your Insurance Agent Do For You?

Beyond selling us our insurance coverage, our insurance agent must answer this question. This presentation shows how to choose an insurance agent and tells what your agent should do for you beyond the basics of selling you insurance.

"Sue Thy Neighbor"

This presentation looks at the growing number of lawsuits and awards and how the resulting costs affect everyone in the U.S. It also gives several potential solutions to this problem that is reaching epidemic proportions.

How a Bill Becomes a Law

The legislative process can be extremely complicated. This presentation addresses some of the inside information on how the legislature works and how the actual process is different from what is presented in textbooks.

Crash, Bang! You've Just Had an Accident

Do you know what to do if you have an accident, or other insurance claim? This presentation tells what to do when you have an insurance claim, and explains how your insurance company should assist in the event of a claim.

Indiana State Legislative Insurance Issues

Many times what happens in the Indiana State Legislature can have a large effect on the insurance industry and its Indiana consumers. Hear what the "hot" insurance issues are and how they could impact the insurance industry, and your insurance rates, if they become laws.

The above programs are informational only. The Institute is a trade association and does not market insurance products. One of the Institute's goals is to provide educational services to Hoosiers, resulting in better informed insurance consumers.

To the right is a reply card to facilitate getting speakers lined up for your group at no cost to you other than a postage stamp. Just drop us a line and we'll do the rest!

Questions or comments? Write the Institute, or call Stephen Duff at (317) 464-8125.

HOW TO RESERVE A SPEAKER

It's simple. Complete this speech request card, specifying the topic you would like to have presented to your group. Then just stamp and mail it to the Institute. We will send you a confirmation letter which includes the speaker's name and biographical information that can be used for his/her introduction at your meeting. Presentations are available at no cost.

Please send the request card at least four weeks in advance of your meeting date!

If you need more than one request card copy the attached one and place it in an envelope or call the Institute for additional cards.

SPEAKER REQUEST CARD

Yes, We would like to schedule a speaker for _____ our group.

Subject (check one)
- ☐ How to Save Money on Your Auto Insurance
- ☐ How to Save Money on Insuring Your Home
- ☐ What Your Insurance Agent Should Do For You
- ☐ Sue Thy Neighbor
- ☐ How a Bill Becomes a State Law
- ☐ Crash, Bang! You've Just Had an Accident
- ☐ Indiana State Legislative Insurance Issues

Group Name _____

Group Size _____

Meeting Date _____

Meeting Time _____

Meeting Place (address): _____

City _____ State _____ Zip _____

Telephone: ( ) _____

Contact Person _____

Address _____

City _____ State _____ Zip _____

Telephone (home) ( ) _____ (office) ( ) _____

(For Office Use Only)
Speaker _____
Contact Date _____

Another viewpoint on marketing your bureau

Let's face it. Everyone sells something, whether directly or indirectly, subtly or aggressively. Through your speakers bureau, you sell the services of your agency and how those services benefit the community.

Your clients are those who use those services and those donors whose financial contributions lend support. Potential clients are those listening to your presentations. Therefore, many of the rules of customer service and good salesmanship apply to your situation. Salesmanship is part of your public relations efforts, and word-of-mouth is a powerful tool for salespeople of all kinds.

In **Word-of-Mouth Marketing**, Jerry Wilson explains how to harness and direct the power of others' recommendations for your service. The following outline lists his 12 rules for Word-of-Mouth marketing:

1. You must have a good product or service to use Word-of-Mouth Marketing strategies--otherwise, you'll just be spreading bad news.

2. The Rule of 3-33. For every 3 people willing to tell a positive story about an experience with your company (or agency), there are 33 others who will tell a horror story.

3. Listen to your Insider Talk! What your employees/staffers say about your service can make it or break it.
continued on next page

4. Identify and cultivate your Champions, those big hitters who will spread the word for you.

5. Word-of-Mouth Marketing ultimately depends on the quality of your customer service.

6. Word-of-Mouth Marketing cuts across every organizational and operational division.

7. The difference between operating a business and operating to generate Word-of-Mouth can be summed up in a word--Attitude.

8. Blow your customers away by exceeding their every expectation.

9. Bellow or beg, if you must, but at all costs, let your customers, clients, and champions know you want their complaints.

10. Catch your employees generating positive Word-of-Mouth and reward them for it.

11. An organization's leaders must commit to active, committed, proven practices for getting things done.

12. Keep your Word-of-Mouth Marketing campaign plan simple but systematic--streamline everything and orient everything to action!

There is intelligent life beyond the media

Contacting print and broadcast media is the first idea in most publicists' minds. But there are indeed other outlets that may add to your efforts, or even surpass the conventional means. Here are some options:

- Let your members or contributors know about your speakers bureau. Make announcements at meetings or distribute information in a special mailing or in your newsletter. Ask them to help locate sources. Rely on them often, and think of your publicity effort as an awareness process that needs periodic emphasis for the group.

- Contact service and professional groups, clubs, schools, and/or churches. The Yellow Pages may include a listing for many of these. Alternatives for finding the addresses and phones of these organizations might be the chamber of commerce or the library.

  One source of interest is Kiwanis International, which has a national listing of speakers willing to appear before individual Kiwanis clubs. Each club's program chair can then call the national headquarters for these suggestions.

- Let your local chamber of commerce know about your efforts. Often people looking for speakers will contact this source for leads and recommendations.

- Send a release or call the local library. Many libraries keep files on such sources and provide the information to interested patrons. You can also post flyers in the library or in other appropriate locations.

- Determine your target market, then go after it. Do you want to reach people in specific industries or corporations? Is your market involved in the school system or in unions? Call the groups affiliated with your target segment, whether it is a leading manufacturer or the nearest elementary school.

- Check with the United Way office in your area. If your group is supported by United Way, many regional offices maintain a listing of speakers who address issues of concern to the agency. When a request for a speaker comes in, the UW office then has your name on file.

- Ask your volunteer speakers to locate an outlet for their presentation. For example, someone who is a member of the local Rotary could contact that group for an assignment. Speakers also could inquire about other sources from family members or friends.

One more step

Follow up your initial mailing to groups, and even the media if appropriate, with a phone call. Keep your tone friendly and helpful and the listener will respond. For a general release, you probably will not want to bother a busy editor. If there is a possibility of a feature article, you might. Remember not to waste the staff's time.

In addition, continue your follow-up with those groups that have made requests on a regular basis. Since they were interested before, they might be again or want information on a related topic.

Summary: Publicizing your bureau's effort is vital to its usefulness. In all your publicity, whether through the media or in other outlets, aim for your targeted markets.

Resources

Kiwanis International, 3636 Woodview Trace, Indianapolis, IN 46268-3196. The phone is 317-875-8755. Contact your local Kiwanis club also.

Gale Directory of Publications and Broadcast Media lists most of the country's media outlets by city and state. (Detroit, Gale Research, 1991).

Guerilla PR: How You Can Wage an Effective Publicity Campaign Without Going Broke, by Michael Levine (New York, NY, Harper Business, 1993).

Marketing Strategies for Nonprofit Organizations, by Siri N. Espy (Chicago, IL, Lyceum Books, 1993).

Word-of-Mouth Marketing, by Jerry Wilson, (New York, NY, John Wiley & Sons, Inc., 1991).

Marketing Workbook for Nonprofit Organizations, by Gary Stern (St. Paul, MN, Amherst H. Wilder Foundation, 1990).

Afterword

Perhaps one of my own experiences best illustrates the effectiveness of sending speakers out into the community. I had been involved with one local charity group for a few years, had discussed the agency and its work with my husband, and shared written material with him. However, it wasn't until a speaker from that group came to talk before his Kiwanis club that he tuned into the message. (This also may be a case of marital communications gone awry.) The point, however, is that, though he didn't tune into my relaying of information, he did listen to an interesting speaker behind a podium who exuded a sense of authority and knowledge.

A speakers bureau augments your communications efforts. It also provides an opportunity to reach busy people who may never take the time to read your newsletter, but who do attend meetings for personal or professional enhancement.

Like all new projects, creating a speakers bureau seems like a lot of work. Once you have all the elements in place, however, you can establish a routine that only needs occasional fine-tuning. With the new contacts and public support your bureau can generate, you will find the work is worth it.

Appendix A

Analysis of speech construction

The following speech about creativity is one that I gave to a group of entrepreneurs. The objective of the speech was to encourage them to nuture their innate creativity. The speech is intended to be more conversational than written essay so there may be a few incomplete sentences and other rule-breaking phrases.

Explanatory statements about the construction of the speech have been printed in bold face and appear throughout the context.

The introduction is intended to give a brief description of my work and to connect with others in the audience.

Many of you know that I work as a writer/photographer and publisher of a small magazine called **The Good Life**. I chose this type of work because it does allow me to explore my creativity-to use the creative process in a large majority of my work. But I became particularly interested in studying the creative process when I started meeting people who did not have a job that one would stereotype as creative, but still had this amazing capacity for creative thoughtfor creative problem solving. Yet they would always point to me as being the creative one simply because of my work. I discovered that no one has a monolopy on creativity.

We all have an innate creativity that's what helped us learn to tie our shoes, to make a crown of flowers from dandelions, to learn how to handle the bully on the playground. But somewhere during the time that we are growing up, many of us learn to bury a lot of those creative thoughts. We learn to color within the lines or to paint zebras black and white instead of red and purple. So it becomes more difficult to tap into our creative resources.

The following quote helps substantiate my opinion and shows that I've done my research.

Psychologist Abraham Maslow describes creativity as a fundamental characteristic, inherent in human nature. His findings indicate that each of us can claim our birthright and utilize the potential for creativity we as a species enjoy if we are willing to exert the effort.

Many researchers agree that creativity is a learnable skill.

At this point, I distribute a sheet relating to the nature of leadership.

It is interesting to note on the sheet on the nature of leadership that one of the top characteristics of leaders is creativity. That Leaders will become more innovative, develop the habit of spontaneity and encourage free thinking and risk taking, both in themselves and others.

Speechwriters refer to the following as a call to action.

As entrepreneurs, we have to be innovative, spontaneous and willing to take risks and therefore must employ creative thinking in all aspects of our work.

But sometimes a problem just seems to have no solution. We think, we pry, we ask other people's opinions, but we still only see questions and not answers. When you find yourself thinking along those lines, then stop and remember this quote by Willis Harman, author of Higher Creativity: '"Each of us has the capacity to become much more than we think we can be if we chose to stop believing otherwise."

And there are various techniques that can tap into that capacity--to nuture that innate creativity.

The following story I used to help illustrate why creative thought is important to the business person.

The way I try to handle problems is not to obsess. My husband, for example, is obsessive about working out a problem. He was trying to find his calculator the other night. Looked all over in all the normal places--couldn't find it. Finally, he had to rest because he couldn't think of where else to look. He sat down to talk to me--watch a little TV. Within a few minutes, he remembered where the calculator was. I try not to spend time like that.

Now we start to look at ways to enhance our creativity.

Be aware of the proble--all the aspects of the problem--then disassociate yourself from the problem. Go do housework, draw, file, or work on another project. Most of the time it works and I find a solution to the problem. Or I might write about the problem and during the process of writing, some insight will appear.

Another way to insight is to encourage active questioning as a thinking mode and to make it an integral part of our activities. We can do this by setting aside a small amount of time each week to review our prior's week's experience by asking questions about them. It's an investment of about 15-30 minutes.

Another method is through images or word associations. Each idea or experience we store contains hundreds, possibly thousands, of associations that can enter into combination with each other to enhance our creative potential. The more mental associations we can make, the more creative potential we have.

One way we can gather these associations is a method that John H. McMurphy has termed as Nuclear Shorthand. I thought we might have some fun by practicing this together.

First I explain the concept of nuclear shorthand, present a way that we can apply it and then allot time for the audience to practice.

The first step in nuclear shorthand is to identify an idea, thought or problem you wish to explore. I'd like to suggest that we come with a theme or slogan for an upcoming Network event. In August, the Network is honoring women who serve in key positions in local art organizations. What are the commonalties of women in the arts and women in business?

In nuclear shorthand, Draw an oval in the middle of a piece of paper and place a key word identifying the question or problem. From that beginning point, you generate various idea streams from that nucleus. Remember to avoid evaluating as you explore. An idea that seems ridiculous may just be the breakthrough you need to find the solution. Then continue until you feel that you have exhausted the idea. Go on to the next stream.

Explore these idea streams. What initial thoughts or impressions do you have about the item. Any items contain or produce an emotional response? Frequently occurring items? Items that immediately grab your attention or strike you as important?

I allot time for questions about the concept. They then tried the technique in small groups while I observed and helped whenever someone seemed to be blocked.

The beginning of the end. The end summarizes the main point of the speech and encourages a plan of action for the listeners.

There are many other methods that you use to help stimulate your creativity. The important thing is to find a method that works for you. Creativity is an essential part of our physical and emotional make-up and it plays an important role for anyone in business.

I distributed a list of books on creativity at the end of the presentation so that they could explore the idea further if they desired.

The next speech is one developed by
The Insurance Institute of Indiana
followed by an outline of that same speech.

Study those elements that grab your attention and ask yourself why.

Speech developed by Insurance Institute of Indiana

Filing An Auto Insurance Claim: How a Claim Becomes a Check

In our society, it is almost a given that insurance is needed to assure our financial well-being and our piece of mind.

However, few things conjure up as much confusion for consumers as does insurance. It is one of the few things we purchase that we cannot taste, touch, smell, feel or conserve. We only gain benefit from our purchase if and when some future event happens, an event that we hope never occurs.

An explanation of how insurance is designed to work and an explanation of the claims process will help you understand the process of insurance.

How Insurance Works

In concept, the insurance system and the insurance mechanism is very simple. In practice, however, it is most complex.

In short, the insurance contract (policy) agrees to do simply one thing--pay money. It promises to pay that money when, and if, certain things occur, and subject to certain conditions.

The insurance mechanism recognizes that we all have risks of possible catastrophic financial loss from such things as accidents, sickness, death, fire, etc. The insurance industry knows. based on historical data, that only 10 to 20 of every 100 policies sold during a given year will result in a claim or loss. It does not know, however, which 10 to 20 will result in claims.

Consequently, the purpose of insurance is to collect enough money, on an equitable basis, from the masses of people in order to have enough money to pay for the losses of the few. In the process, its objective is to make a reasonable profit, since it does operate as a private enterprise.

Taking The Mystery Out Of Auto Insurance Claims

In movies and TV, everyone loves a good mystery. But when something as upsetting as an auto accident occurs in your life, not knowing what is going to happen can be annoying, or frightening.

Few people know how an auto insurance claim is handled once they've filed one. Yet, people know they don't have to worry about claims, because seventyfive percent of all auto insurance claims are paid in thirty days, many much sooner than that.

Studies show that when customers deal with their own insurer, eighty-six percent of them are satisfied with the speed and the amount of the payment. That is a pretty good approval rating.

Claims handling may seem mystifying and not worth learning about...until you or someone you love or know has an accident. Then it pays to know what's going on, especially if there are injuries, or serious damage to the car. Or the crash may be your fault and you may be sued. You'll be depending on your insurance company to protect you.

The possibility of a claim is not remote for any of us. I hope none of you will be included in these numbers, but you should know that this year there will be about thirtyfour million car crashes. About fortyfive million claims will be filed. Insurance companies will pay out approximately sixtyfive billion dollars to settle them.

For the next few minutes, I'd like to explain what companies do with claims, and why they do it.

The claims process starts when you report a loss to your company or agent.

A simple phone call is the usual notice. But in some cities, insurance companies often get their first word of an accident not from the customer, but from a lawyer, who was hired even before the claim was reported.

The claimsperson...they are sometimes called adjusters...will take down the basic information: what happened, who was driving, what car was involved, etc.

The first step the company takes is to verify coverage. In other words, to see that the policy covers what happened. Sometimes it shouldn't.

We verify coverage to make sure that we pay all valid claims, but only valid claims. We can't give away the store by paying anything and everything, or the price of everybody's insurance would skyrocket.

The claimsperson can also explain to you exactly what's covered and what isn't. If you have a question or aren't sure about your policy, don't be shy about asking questions. The claimsperson is there to answer them.

After they have verified coverage, companies try to contact you as soon as possible. . .by phone, in person or by writing. . .to let you know they're working on your claim. They also want to calm any anxiety you may feel or offer help and advice.

If repairing your car is going to take a long time, your policy may include coverage for a rental car.

If the claim looks like it's a difficult one, companies often make advance partial payments even before they have investigated the claim.

You may be asked to sign a form acknowledging that the partial payment will be deducted from the final settlement, Contrary to what you may have heard, signing this form does not jeopardize your rights in any way. The company is still obligated to pay your claim fully and properly.

The next step is to investigate the claim.

This could take hours or weeks. Normally, most claims are handled very quickly. As I said a moment ago, three-fourths of all auto claims are paid in a matter of weeks.

But when we have serious or complicated claims, especially those with injuries, the investigation has to be more thorough. We use elaborate checklists to investigate a crash. We look at road conditions, condition of the cars and the drivers, the presence of alcohol or drugs, identification of victims, witnesses, police officers, doctors, paramedics, and more.

This is where delays can occur. It takes time to interview people. Conflicting stories may be told, and sometimes, people are reluctant to cooperate. Uninsured motorists or hit-and-run drivers have to be traced, if possible.

During the investigation phase, you may be asked to go to a claim center or make your car available to a damage appraiser. This is the time we ask you for repair estimates, bills, receipts, and other proofs of loss. And you are asked to sign proof of loss forms, or medical authorization forms to allow us to obtain medical records, if there has been an injury to someone.

There are other reasons why a claim could be delayed as the investigation widens and more questions are asked.

The first is the prevalence of fraud.

It's an unattractive comment on Americans, but it's also an undeniable fact that some people cheat. Fifteen percent of all car thefts are fraudulent. A recent study in Florida showed that 13 percent of the claims paid were fraudulent.

We all pay the high cost of fraud. Staged thefts, faked accidents, phony injuries, and other scams add at least eight billion dollars a year to the public's auto insurance bill. For the average consumer, that's about fifty dollars of your premium. It's really a national scandal.

Claimspersons have to be alert for possible fraud every time they handle a claim.

Suspicious ones get special handling. They may be referred to the company's own Special Investigative Unit, or they may be sent to the National Auto Theft Bureau or the Insurance Crime Prevention Institute. These organizations save the public millions of dollars every year by uncovering phony claims.

Companies also work closely with police agencies, but they can't catch all of the fraud.

Another reason a claim will sometimes be held up is lawsuits.

In our country today, suing each other over auto accidents is a growth industry. Between 1977 and 1988, the use of lawyers in auto cases shot up sixty percent.

We're at the point now that half of every dollar we pay out for auto accident injuries goes--not to doctors and hospitals--but to lawyers and court awards.

Claimspersons know that every paper they handle, every statement they make may end up in court. So they scrupulously build up a written record to preserve possible evidence. Our claims file may eventually include dozens of reports, tape recordings, videotape, police reports, medical charts, and much more.

The most regrettable aspect of this lawsuit craze is that it's so unnecessary. The vast majority of claims are going to be paid fully in less than thirty days. Hiring a lawyer often only slows up the process and makes the claim more expensive. The lawyer is naturally going to try to increase the amount of the claim, to justify being hired, and to cover his or her fees.

The company has legal expenses, too, which we have to pay even if we win the case. In the end, all these expenses drive up insurance premiums for all of us.

I'm not saying that you shouldn't retain a lawyer if you truly think you need one. That's a basic civil right. But many people hire lawyers even before the insurance company has had a chance to investigate the accident and offer a payment. Much of the lawyering that takes place today is based on people's fear and mistaken idea that their legitimate claims won't be paid. And that simply is not true.

Remember, this year there are going to be about forty-five million claims paid. . .about sixty-five billion dollars. We couldn't be distributing that kind of money if we were fighting claims unduly.

There's one more reason that a claim could be complicated. It usually doesn't happen, but sometimes claimants are asked questions about the accident after they've received payment and they wonder why.

If an investigation shows that other persons or insurance companies are responsible, your company will generally pay you, then collect that money from the other party. This is known as subrogation.

The other parties sometimes resist paying, so the matter may be turned over to an attorney. That keeps the claim file active, and you could be contacted for some additional information long after you received a check.

After the investigation is complete, the next step in claims handling is the settlement. Routinely, a week or two after the accident, you, your medical providers or the auto repair shop receive the check.

Sometimes, though, problems remain. The company will try to negotiate an informal settlement of the differences with you. If that fails, we may suggest arbitration by an independent third party. If we still can't get together, the case may go to court. But, as I said, insurance companies don't like lawsuits and they try hard to avoid them.

The final step for the company is something called reserving. It doesn't apply to all the claims we settle easily and quickly. But on complex claims that are going to be open a while, the law requires companies to estimate the cost and earmark enough money, called reserves, to pay the total expenses.

Claimspersons take into account factors like the accumulation of medical bills, inflation, lost wages, the claimant's suffering and inconvenience. In case of death, the loss of future earnings and companionship are considered.

A Word About Homeowners Claims

The process for a claim involving a homeowners loss is basically the same as one for auto insurance. The most important thing that you need to do is to contact your agent or company as soon as possible.

If the claim is on your home, such as for a fire or other loss, the company will want to get your money to you to start repairs or rebuilding as soon as possible, especially if there is extensive damage.

A helpful document to have in the event of a homeowners loss is a home inventory. This is a listing of all of the items that you own and their approximate values. This should be done before a loss and kept with your homeowners policy outside of the home in a safety deposit box, away from possible damage from a catastrophe. This document will help speed along the claim process because if you experience a major loss, chances are that you will not remember everything you had in every room of your home.

Conclusion

The most important thing to remember is that fundamentally every insurance company has the privilege of doing business in this country for one reason, and one reason only. . .to pay claims. If they don't do that and do it well, they're not going to be around long. A quarter of the industry's employees. . .about a hundred and forty thousand men and women. . .handle claims, and they are there to help you.

I have a brochure entitled *How to File An Insurance Claim* that takes you step by step through the process that I just explained.

Thank you. Any questions?

Speech Outline

Filing An Auto Insurance Claim: How a Claim Becomes a Check

I. Introduction

Insurance is a needed commodity in our society. Few things, however, conjure up as much confusion for consumers as does insurance.

Insurance is unusual in that we only gain a benefit from our purchase if and when some future event occurs, one that we hope will never occur.

II. How insurance works.

The concept is simple. In practice, it is complex.

    A. The insurance contract (policy) agrees to do one thing pay money, if and when certain things occur and conditions are met.

    B. The insurance mechanism realizes that we all have risks of possible catastrophic financial loss.

Based on historical data, only 10 to 20 of every 100 policies sold in a given year will result in a claim it is not known, however, which 10 to 20 will result in claims.

C. Purpose of insurance:

1. To collect enough money from the masses to pay for the losses of the few.

2. In the process, its objective is to make a reasonable profit.

III. Taking the mystery out of auto insurance claims.

A. To many, the auto insurance claim process is an unknown. Most people don't worry about is until they are in an accident.

B. When an accident occurs. it is helpful to know how the process works especially in the event of serious injuries or damage to the car.

More importantly. if a crash is your fault. you may be sued and your insurance company will defend you.

C. Here are some statistics on auto accidents:

1. There are 34 million car crashes annually.

2. 45 million claims are filed from these accidents.

3. Insurance companies pay out $65 billion to settle them.

IV. The auto accident claims process.

A. Notify your agent or company as soon as possible after an accident this starts the claims process.

1. An adjuster will record basic information: what happened, who was driving, cars involved. etc.

B. The first step the insurance company takes is to verify coverage and see if the policy covers what happened.

C. After coverage is verified, the policyholder will be notified that the company is working on the claim.

D. If a difficult claim arises, companies often make advance partial payments before the claim is totally investigated.

E. Companies then investigate the claim, which could take hours, or weeks. Most claims are handled quickly. 75 percent of all claims are paid within a month.

F. Serious claims, especially those with injuries, require a more thorough investigation.

1. Things examined include road conditions, condition of the cars and drivers, presence of alcohol or drugs, witnesses, police officers and doctors involved, etc.

2. Delays can occur in this type of investigation.

G. Other reasons for claims delays:

1. Incidence of fraud.

   a. 15 percent of all car thefts are fraudulent.

   b. 13 percent of auto claims paid are fraudulent.

   c. Fraudulent claims add $8 billion to the public's auto insurance bill, which equates to about $50 for the average consumer's annual auto premium.

   d. Companies do their best to fight fraud, but it is difficult to detect all incidences of fraud.

2. Lawsuits.

   a. Between 1977 and 1988, the use of lawyers in auto cases increased 60 percent.

   b. 50 percent of every dollar paid in claims goes to lawyers and court awards.

   c. Most of the time a lawyer is not needed in a case. They often serve to slow down the process and make claims more expensive.

   d. Many people hire a lawyer in these situations because of the mistaken idea that their claims won't be paid by their insurance company. This simply is not true.

H. The final step is settlement.

   1. Within a few weeks, at the maximum, either you or the auto repair facility and medical providers will receive a check, barring any delays or problems.

V. A word about homeowners claims.

   A. Process is similar. Most important thing is to contact your agent or company as soon as possible.

   B. With extensive damage, company will get money to you as soon as possible to start repair or rebuilding your home.

   C. Home inventory can speed claims process.

      1. Is a listing of all belongings in each room of the home.

      2. Should be kept with homeowners policy outside of the home in a safety deposit box.

VI. Conclusion.

   A. The brochure, *How to file an Auto Insurance Claim* will take you step by step through the process that I just explained.

   B. Remember, the fundamental reason that insurance exists is to pay policyholder claims. Any company that does not do this will not be in business very long.

   Thank YOU. Any questions?

Appendix B

Summary of Additional Resources

(Structure and Organization)

How to Write a Successful Business Plan, by Julie Brooks and Barry A. Stevens (New York, NY, American Management Association, 1987).

Positioning: The Battle for Your Mind, by Al Ries and Jack Trout (New York, NY, McGraw-Hill, 1981).

Getting Started on Strategic Planning, by John M. Bryson in cassette form, (San Francisco, CA, Jossey-Bass, Inc., 1991).

Doing Well While Doing Good: The Marketing Link Between Business & Nonprofit Causes, by Lawrence L. Embley (Englewood Cliffs, NJ, Prentice Hall, 1993).

You Are the Message: Secrets of Master Communicators, by Roger Ailes with Jon Kraushar (New York, NY, Dow Jones-Irwin, 1989).

(Working with Speakers)

Painless Public Speaking, by Sharon Anthony Bower (Englewood Cliffs, NJ, Prentice Hall, 1981).

Secrets of Motivation: How to Get & Keep Volunteers & Paid Staff!, by Sue Vineyard (Downers Grove, IL, Heritage Arts, 1991).

Recruiting Volunteers: A Guide for Non-Profits, by Mary Ann Burke and Carl Liljenstolpe (Los Altos, CA, Crisp Publications, 1992).

Leadership and Management of Volunteer Programs, by James C. Fisher (San Francisco, CA, Jossey-Bass, Inc., 1993).

Speak and Grow Rich, by Dottie Walters and Lilly Walters (Englewood Cliffs, NJ, Prentice Hall, 1989.

Megatrends and Volunteerism, by Sue Vineyard, published by Heritage Arts Publishing, a division of VMSystems, 1993).

101 Tips for Volunteer Recruitment, by Steve MCurley and Sue Vineyard, published by Heritage Arts Publishing, 1988).

(Writing the Speech)

The Public Speakers Bible, by Stuart Turner (Wellinborough, Thorsons Publishing Group, 1988).

The Art of Plain Talk, by Rudolf Flesch (New York, NY, Harper & Brothers, 1946).

The Quick and Easy Way to Effective Speaking, by Dale Carnegie (New York, NY, Pocket Books, 1977).

Instant Eloquence: a lazy man's guide to public speaking, by James C. Humes (New York, NY, Harper & Row, 1973).

Roles Speakers Play, by James C. Humes (New York, NY, Harper & Row, 1976).

(Publicity and Marketing)

Gale Directory of Publications and Broadcast Media lists most of the country's media outlets by city and state. (Detroit, Gale Research, 1991).

Guerilla PR: How You Can Wage an Effective Publicity Campaign Without Going Broke, by Michael Levine (New York, NY, Harper Business, 1993).

Marketing Strategies for Nonprofit Organizations, by Siri N. Espy (Chicago, IL, Lyceum Books, 1993).

Word-of-Mouth Marketing, by Jerry Wilson, (New York, NY, John Wiley & Sons, Inc., 1991).

Marketing Workbook for Nonprofit Organizations, by Gary Stern (St. Paul, MN, Amherst H. Wilder Foundation, 1990).

Index

Ailes, Robert, 3-7

American Society of Association Executives, ii

The Art of Plain Talk, 3-8

Better Business Meetings, iii

Biographical data, 4-11

Brochures, 4-11, 13, 14

Business plan
 advantages, 1-1
 questions to consider, 1-2, 1-3

Canned speeches, 3-1

Checklist for Presentation, 1-7, 1-8

Confirmation letter, 1-6, 11

Doing Well While Doing Good: The Marketing Link Between Business & Nonprofit Causes, 1-17

Economy, Peter, iii

Elements of the speech, 3-1, 2, 3

Engagement Reminder, 1-11

Evaluation
 Presentation forms, 1-12, 1-13
 Speakers, 1-14

Fact sheet, 4-11

Francis, Ray, 2-7

Gale Directory of Publications and Broadcast Media, 4-19

Getting Started on Strategic Planning, 1-17

Guerilla PR: How You Can Wage an Effective Publicity Campaign Without Going Broke, 4-20

Herzberg, Frederick, 2-10

How to Write a Successful Business Plan, 1-17

Instant Eloquence: a lazy man's guide to public speaking, 3-8

Insurance Institute of Indiana, 1-3, 1-15, 16
 sample of brochure, 4-13, 14

Indiana University Center on Philanthropy, 2-10

Kiwanis International, 4-1, 17, 18

Leadership and Management of Volunteer Programs, 2-12

League of Women Voters of the United States, 2-2

Lock Haven Express, 4-5

Marketing Strategies for Nonprofit Organizations, 4-19

Marketing Workbook for Nonprofit Organizations, 4-19

Meeting Professionals International, ii

Meeting Outlook Survey, ii

Motivating Volunteers, 2-7, 8

Motviational Hygiene Theory, 2-10

Megatrends and Volunteerism, 2-12

Nelson, Robert B., iii

News release, 4-1, 3, 4, 5, 6, 7, 8, 12

101 Tips for Volunteer Recruitment, 2-12

PR Kit, 4-11, 12

Painless Public Speaking, 2-4, 12

Platform skills, 1-2, 3, 4, 3-4, 5, 6

Positioning statement, 1-5, 4-2

Positioning: The Battle for Your Mind, 1-17

Problems in communications, 3-7

Public Service Announcement, 4-9, 10

The Public Speakers Bible, 3-8

The Quick and Easy Way to Effective Speaking, 3-8

Recognition ideas, 2-8

Recruiting, 2-5

Recruiting Volunteers: A Guide for Non-Profits, 2-12

Roles Speakers Play, 3-8

Speakers bureau
   audience, 1-4
   definition, v
   image, ii, iv, 1-3
   organizational tips, 1-5, 6, 9
   participants, 1-4

Secrets of Motivation: How to Get & Keep Volunteers & Paid Staff!, 2-12

Speak and Grow Rich, 2-12

Speech elements, 3-2, 3, 4

Standardized forms, 1-6, 11, 12, 13

Storytelling, 2-3

Toastmasters International, 2-6, 10

Visual aids, 2-11, 3-4

Volunteer Action Center, 2-6, 10

Volunteers, 1-5, 6, 2-1, 2, 3, 5

Wilson, Jerry, 4-15, 16

Word of Mouth Marketing, 4-15, 16, 19

You Are the Message: Secrets of Master Communicators, 1-17

An Invitation

I hope this book has provided all the information that you need to get your speakers bureau operational. Any further questions you have can be directed to me at
 9220 N. College Avenue, Indianapolis, IN 46240
 Phone: 317-844-6869
 Fax: 317-844-0669
 e-mail: horvath@in.net
 Compuserve: 74117,260.
 Home page address is:
 http://www.in.net/resource/sprdword.html

I'd also enjoy hearing your success stories and any problems you may have encountered.

Sincerely,

Terri Horvath

Scheduled for publication early 1996

Fund-raising successes:
Case studies of 50+ fund-raising events
by Terri Horvath

Before you venture into another mediocre fund-raising event or even a failure, read how over 50 fund-raising coordinators make their events successful.

The book contains a detailed summary of each event outlined by the people who know what works and what doesn't.

You will find an outline of each event explaining:
- three major keys to its success
- income and expenses
- personnel involved
- planning schedule
- history and description of event
- target markets

and much more.

Easy-to-follow symbols indicate various needs by the sponsor and functional details, such as those organizations which use a strong volunteer force or those events that generate large profits. These icons are designed to help the readers concentrate on suggestions right for their own organizations.

Profit from other's experience by ordering Fund-raising successes.

Order by calling **1-317-844-6869**, or by completing the order form on the next page.

Order form

Publishing Resources, 9220 N. College Avenue, Indianapolis, IN 46240
317-844-6869   Fax: 317-844-0669

Please send me the following:
Spread the Word:
How to promote nonprofit groups with a network of speakers
Price: $14.95
Number of copies_____
Fund-raising successes: case studies of 50 + fund-raising events
Price $14.95
Number of copies_____

Add 5% Sales tax for Indiana addresses
Add shipping fee of $3.00 for first book and 75 cents for each additional book. Surface shipping may take three to four weeks.

I wish to charge the amount to my
MasterCard Account number_____

Visa Account number_____

Expiration Date_____

Signature_____

Total amount enclosed_____

send to

Name_____

Street Address_____

City_____

State_____Zip_____

For phone orders, please have your Master Card or Visa charge card number ready. **Phone: 317-844-6869**